Kittens

Understanding and Caring for Your Pet

Written by
Claire Horton-Bussey

Mason Crest
450 Parkway Drive, Suite D
Broomall, PA 19008
www.masoncrest.com
Developed and produced by Mason Crest

Printed and bound in the United States of America.

First printing
9 8 7 6 5 4 3 2 1

Series ISBN: 978-1-4222-3691-8
ISBN: 978-1-4222-3700-7
ebook ISBN: 978-1-4222-8092-8

Words in bold are explained in the glossary on page 127.

QR CODES AND LINKS TO THIRD PARTY CONTENT

Understanding and Caring for Your Pet

Aquarium
Cats
Dog Training
Ferrets
Gerbils
Goldfish

Guinea Pigs
Hamsters
Kittens
Parakeets
Puppies
Rabbits

 Educational Videos: Readers can view videos by scanning our QR codes, providing them with additional educational content to supplement the text. Examples include news coverage, moments in history, speeches, iconic moments, and much more!

 Words to Understand: These words with their easy-to-understand definitions will increase the reader's understanding of the text, while building vocabulary skills.

Contents

Foreword 8

Introduction 12

Taming the wild cat 16

How many? 22

Which breed? 24

      Bengal 26
      Maine Coon Cat 28
      Burmese 30
      Manx 32
      Siamese 34
      Persian 36
      Mixed breed 38

Where to get your kitten 40

Boy or girl? 46

Preparing your home 48

Essential equipment 54

Litter box training 68

Family introductions 74

Outdoors or in? 82

Behavior 98

Food 102

Grooming 110

Health 116

Vacations 124

Find out more / Words to understand 126

Index 128

Foreword

Kittens are fantastic fun—playful, funny, loving, and energetic. It's easy to spend hours just watching them, playing with them, petting them, and enjoying them to the fullest. They don't stay kittens, of course—though many remain young at heart throughout their lives.

The very best news is that kittens grow up to be cats, which are just as beautiful and, in many ways, better companions. Adult cats spend longer in one place—particularly laps—than crazy little kits that race all over the house, pouncing on anything that moves and scaling your curtains or trouser legs for fun, hell-bent on seeing how many of their nine lives they can use up!

The great advantage of getting a kitten rather than an adult cat is that you can mold him to your home and family, **socializing** him thoroughly to ensure he is confident around children, dogs, other cats and so on.

You don't have this luxury with an adult cat, and have to hope that someone else has already done the hard work for you.

Compared with some pets, kittens are simple to care for. They don't need expensive equipment, as some reptiles do, and they don't need to be taken for walks, like a dog. But just because they are independent creatures, it doesn't mean they are entirely self-sufficient; a kitten will need you to play with him, train him, groom him, pet him, and simply spend time with him.

As well as the time commitment, it is also important to ensure that you can afford the life-long responsibility that cat ownership entails, including food and vet bills, and also that everyone in the household is in agreement about sharing the home with a feline.

This book will help you all understand how to raise and care for a kitten throughout his life, ensuring he is happy and healthy—and a joy to share your home with.

Introduction

Cats are one of the most popular pets in the world. There are an estimated 60 million pet cats in the United States. More than 90 percent of these are mixed breed cats.

According to the Pet Food Manufacturers' Association, people choose a cat as a pet for companionship and love, and because they are easy to care for and get along with other species.

Cats and kittens are very adaptable and can be found in all sorts of households—single homes, busy families, older couples, country or city, apartment or house. Provided they are safe from danger and can have their basic care needs met, a kitten will thrive in many different living environments.

Unlike dogs, cats can be left for hours while their owners work, though it's advisable to spend at least a few days with a new kitten, to settle him in and supervise him. In addition, cats are small and do not require a large home or yard. In fact, most cats are just fine living entirely indoors, as long as they are given adequate opportunities to express their natural behaviors (hunting, climbing, scratching, etc.) indoors.

Their size also ensures that kittens and cats can be picked up and carried easily—it's far easier taking a cat to the vet than a reluctant St. Bernard dog, for example—they don't require huge bowls of food, and they fit on a lap perfectly well for a cuddle!

Kittens come in many colors and patterns, and, for those who would like even more choice, there are many **pedigree** breeds to choose from. There really is a kitten for almost every taste!

Taming the Wild Cat

Watch a cat playing in the garden or stalking a toy on the rug and it's not difficult to see where his origins lie. He may have been domesticated for several thousand years, but he still retains many features of his wild ancestor, the African wildcat.

The cat family (Felidae) is a varied group, and emerged during the Miocene period, which was about 10 million to 11 million years ago. These feline ancestors eventually evolved into eight major groups, including the Panthera (lions, tiger, and other big cats), and Felis (smaller wildcats).

The domesticated cat's story began with the agricultural revolution about 10,000 to 12,000 years ago, when humans began storing their crops, but rats and mice posed a serious threat to the stores, and a pack of rats could mean starvation for the humans. Fortunately, cats were equally as attracted to the granaries—not for the grain but for the easy rodent hunting! People welcomed the cats' help in getting rid of the rodents, and, over time, the cats became less fearful of humans and more relaxed around the human settlements.

With a combination of some kind of genetic mutation occurring, together with selective breeding (people-tolerant cats in the settlement mating with others of a similar character), the cat became domesticated over time. About 4,000 years ago, the Egyptians began domesticating cats more seriously, and keeping them as pets.

His fortunes have waxed and waned through the ages, from being worshipped in Ancient Egypt to being persecuted in the Middle Ages because of an association with witches, but he is now securely top of our list of favorite pets—a spot he's unlikely to relinquish any time soon.

How Many?

It's often said that cats are solitary creatures, but this isn't true. Yes, cats are lone hunters, unlike some animals that hunt in pairs or packs, but they often choose to live happily in groups. This is evident from watching feral cat groups, where close, lasting relationships can be seen, particularly in the adult females, who help to nurse and raise kittens together.

An only cat in a home will be more than content, provided his needs are met, but many cats can—and do—live happily with one or more of their own kind, particularly if they meet when they are both young. Two kittens are likely to play with each other and bond closely, whereas an older puss may be less tolerant of having his tail stalked and pounced on! The key to success is to ensure both kittens are sociable and friendly, that they each receive plenty of petting, lap-warming, play and quiet time alone, when

they can escape to a snooze spot away from others if they want to.

Most squabbles arise over competition for resources. So ensure that each feline in the home has a litter box, bed, food and water bowl, and perch (somewhere such as a high windowsill). And remember, you also count as a resource, so make sure you give your lap and attention to each puss, too!

Personality also plays a part, of course. Some cats are simply loners and only you will know if your cat would accept a newcomer. Perhaps you have an oldie that has never shared his home with a feline friend and is aggressive to any cat that enters into his territory, or maybe you have a younger, very territorial cat or one that is very nervous and fearful. However, many will accept a new kitten in the home provided the situation is handled carefully. However, the energy of a kitten is more than most adult cats want to deal with. So if you are getting a kitten, whether you already have a cat at home or not, seriously consider doubling up.

With time, they will become increasingly confident around each other, and, in many cases, will be curling up next to each other for a nap before you know it!

Which Breed?

Cats do not have the same diversity as dog breeds. They are fairly uniform in size and appearance—unlike, say, a Chihuahua and an Irish Wolfhound. But there are quite a few breeds with their own distinct looks and personalities. Here are some of the most popular.

Bengal

The Bengal's popularity lies in how similar it looks to small wildcats. And in fact, it is a hybrid of a domestic cat and the Asian leopard cat. Domestic Bengals are four generations or more away from their wild ancestors.

Large, muscular, and with an awesome patterned coat (spotted or marbled tabby in brown, white or silver), the Bengal may look wild, but breeders have worked hard to ensure that early aggression and fear problems have been removed. Nowadays, the Bengal is a friendly, super-smart cat, playful, and energetic, and a loving addition to the family home.

Maine Coon Cat

This native American longhaired breed developed naturally, and without any help from raccoons!

They were originally working cats, and needed that long coat in the hard Northeast winters. They are noted for their intelligence and gentle disposition—and their large size. They come in about 75 different color and pattern combinations.

Burmese

The breed was created by breeding a sealpoint Siamese from Thailand to a female cat that was taken to America from Rangoon, the Burmese capital, in 1930.

Careful subsequent breeding established the breed, though two types have since emerged: the European Burmese (which is more Oriental in appearance, with a slender, athletic body, longer legs, and a more refined face); and the American (which has a shorter nose and rounder skull). Both types have the short, velvety coat, which comes in various colors with tortoiseshell variations. Vocal, clever, and playful, the Burmese loves human company.

Manx

As his name suggests, the Manx cat comes from the Isle of Man, off the northwest coast of Britain. He is most famous for his short or nonexistent tail.

Legend has it that Noah shut the door on the cat's tail when he closed the Ark, but in fact the breed's tail is due to a genetic mutation that occurred naturally at least 300 years ago and was bred into future generations due to the limited gene pool on the island. Manx cats can be any color and pattern and any coat length. A longhaired Manx is also known as a Cymric.

Siamese

One of the oldest pedigreed breeds of domestic cat, dating back to around 1300, the Siamese once roamed the palaces of Siam, as he was considered a treasure of royalty.

Taking the cats out of the country was a crime punishable by death. Fortunately, they did eventually make their way out of what is now Thailand, and have been a firm favorite with cat lovers the world over ever since. This is hardly surprising, given their majestic good looks and incredible character. The show-type Siamese has become very exaggerated in recent decades, but the traditional Siamese type continues to be bred by those who are not such fans of the extreme look of the modern breed. Vocal, active, loving, demanding, and strong-willed, the Siamese is highly intelligent. This cat needs an owner who will give lots of attention, play, and love.

Persian

Like the Siamese, the Persian has also changed dramatically due to the show world and changing tastes. The modern Persian has a much flatter, squashed-in face, a longer, more luxurious coat, and a larger head than its forbears.

Traditional, more moderate-looking Persians can still be found, however, for those who are not fans of the exaggerated type. Regardless of type, grooming is a big part of owning this breed; the coat (which comes in a very wide range of colors and patterns) is thick and long and needs daily brushing. It is just as well, then, that the Persian is so laid-back and enjoys the attention of being pampered. Generally a calm cat, the Persian isn't as energetic as some breeds and loves to snooze on a lap or in a warm bed.

Mixed Breed

A mixed breed cat has no pedigree, but is still 100 percent feline. Mixed breeds typically suffer from fewer genetic health problems than pedigree cats, which have a closed gene pool and are therefore more prone to breed-related health disorders.

Mixed breed kittens are available for adoption everywhere, especially in the spring and fall, when shelters and rescue groups are overrun with kittens. It's yet another great reason to take them home in pairs!

Where to Get Your Kitten

The best place to find a kitten is from a reputable rescue center. Here you will find a good selection of cats of all ages—perhaps even a particular breed—who will have been vet-checked and handled and assessed by experienced staff. This is preferable to buying a kitten from a private ad in a newspaper or from the Internet, where you may not be certain of the animal's health and history, and where the sellers may not offer any post-sale advice and support.

There are many types of rescue organizations. Some rescue dogs and cats (and sometimes rabbits and other small pets, too), some just specialize in cats, and some are dedicated to just one breed, such as the Siamese.

If you want a rescue kitten of a particular breed, you may have to wait quite some time for the right cat to become available, especially in the numerically small breeds, but if you would like a mixed breed, you will have more than enough to choose from. Rescue centers are usually overflowing with beautiful cats and kittens of every description. Some may be there because they have strayed and cannot be reunited with their owners, but most kittens will have either been born in rescue (with mom having been handed in or found as a stray), or found dumped. Some are handed in when people have had a litter and are unable to find the kittens homes.

Every rescue center has its own policies, but you will generally be interviewed, to assess your family and home's suitability and to find out your wants and needs.

Boy or Girl?

Identifying the sex of a kitten can be a tricky business. Hopefully, the breeder/rescue group will have accurately determined if you have a boy or a girl kitten, but it doesn't hurt to check! Even vets get it wrong sometimes, particularly if the youngster is just a few weeks old. It becomes more obvious as the kitten grows, and by the time the kitten is old enough to be brought home, there should be no doubt.

The best way to remember it is to think in terms of punctuation! From behind, with the cat's tail up, the female cat's bottom and genitals will look like an upside-down exclamation mark.

A male cat will look more like a colon (one small circle above another). Also, the gap between the anus and the genitals is shorter in the female than in the male. You might even see a slight swelling just below the anus in a male cat - these are the testicles.

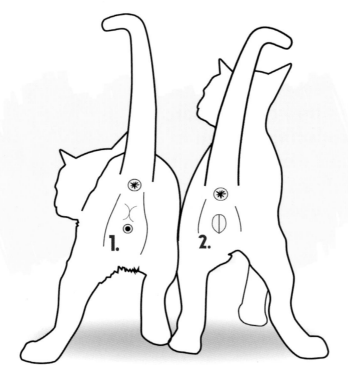

male (tomcat)

1. penile opening (circle)

female (queen)

2. vulva (vertical slit)

Preparing Your Home

Before bringing your kitten home, it's important to prepare a room that puss can call his own. Your bedroom is ideal. Cats, when stressed, seek small hiding places where they can feel safe and protected. Introducing a kitten to your entire home and expecting him to settle in immediately away is asking too much. First, get him used to one room and then, as he gains confidence, he will venture out and start exploring the rest of the house in his own time, returning to his "safe room" if spooked.

Place his bed, litter box, and food and water bowls in the room, making sure the litter box is as far away from the bed and bowls as it can be. (Nobody likes to go to the toilet where they eat!)

Put some toys in the room for him to play with (and for you to play with together when you visit the room), and also put a scratching post inside. Make sure the windows are locked (some smart cats can open windows!) and be sure the room is cat-safe (no **toxic** houseplants, such as Poinsettia or lilies; no irreplaceable heirlooms on a mantelpiece or shelf within the cat's reach, etc).

Next, kitten-proof the rest of the house and garden. Assess each room from a cat's perspective, getting down on your hands and knees if necessary! Don't underestimate the devastation that a kitten can cause in play—whether chasing his own tail, hunting a fly, or testing out how high he can scale your curtains. Put breakable ornaments away or display them in a cabinet with glass doors.

Electrical cables are another hazard. Kittens seem genetically programmed to find dangling wires to play with and chew, so gather up excess electrical wire and fasten it with a cable tie.

Preparing your home for a new cat

You should also discuss with all family members some basic rules to ensure the new kitten's safety:

- The toilet seat should always be put down when not in use, so a curious puss can't jump in and/or drink from the bowl and ingest any harmful cleaning chemicals.

- Windows should be shut/locked and doors kept closed. Screens can be fitted to windows that allow air to enter, but prevent a kitten escaping.

- The dishwasher, washing machine, and dryer doors should be kept shut when not in use and the insides should be checked before they are switched on in case your kitten has crept inside. All chemicals and medicines should be shut away (antifreeze, aspirin, and acetaminophen, for example, can be deadly to cats).

- The shed/garage should always be checked before being locked up, in case your kitten has sneaked inside.

Only use products that are entirely cat-safe in your yard and garden. If you have a pool or pond, these should be covered and ramps should be fitted so that puss can climb out if he falls in.

If you have a dog in the home, set up a baby gate so your kitten can have his safe room to himself, away from any canine attention. In time, and with careful introductions, he will be happy to slip through the gate to be social downstairs, but in the early days, he will want to find his feet and settle in, unbothered by the family dog.

Essential
Equipment

Essential Equipment

A kitten's needs are pretty basic compared with most pets, but there are some essential things you should buy before bringing him home.

Bed

There is a bed to suit every taste and budget. Although you can get ornate four-posters and sofa lounges for cats (yes, really!), most have humbler tastes, preferring a pile of freshly washed laundry washing! A simple, fleecy pad-type bed is a good starting point, or, better still, a hooded cat bed, which will help to make puss feel safe and protected. Place the bed in a corner of the room, or, if it is deep enough, on a windowsill.

Bowls

You will need at least two bowls—one for food and one for water—though four are ideal, so you can wash one set while another set is being used. Choose from glass, ceramic, or stainless steel. Plastic bowls can scratch eventually and become quite abrasive. The design is important: cats prefer to eat from shallow bowls rather than deep ones.

Food

Find out in advance what the kitten is being fed, so you can get a supply before you bring him home.

Litter accessories

You will need a litter box, scoop, a place to dispose of what you scoop, cleaner (unscented dish detergent works well for cleaning the box), and a supply of cat litter. Even a cat who spends some time outside needs a litter box for when he is inside and has to go. (In any case, kittens should not go outside at all until they are at least six months old.)

If you already have a cat, get another box for the newcomer, because many cats will not use a box that is used by another cat. The general rule is as many boxes as there are cats, plus one—so two cats will need three boxes between them.

Get the biggest litter box available. Most boxes are too small, so go for jumbo. Your little kitten will look tiny in it now, but when he grows up, he'll need the bigger bathroom. Just make sure the sides of the box are not too high for him! Some kittens prefer the privacy that a covered box offers, but most prefer a large, open box. Bear in mind that the best way to keep your home smelling sweet is to scoop the box twice a day and to change all the litter regularly. If the litter is very dirty, most cats won't use it and will find a clean corner of the house to relieve them-selves instead!

There are many types of litter—wood-based pellets, paper, clay, silica crystals, lightweight, and the type that forms a scoopable clump when it comes into contact with liquid. Find out what your kitten is used to and get a supply before bringing him home. If you want to change the type of litter, add a little of the new material to the one he's used to already, mix it in, and gradually, over the course of a few days, increase the amount of new to old until you've made the switch.

Tip: If your kitten is fussy about the type of litter he uses, try a fine grain, which many cats prefer.

Identification

Most shelters will microchip the animals in their care before they are sent home, but if you get your kitten from another source, then you may have to arrange for your vet to do it. It is a simple procedure where a small chip, the size of a long grain of rice, is inserted under the skin at the back of the neck, between the shoulder blades. This chip contains a unique number, which will be held on a database with your details. If your kitten becomes lost and is scanned by a reader, you can quickly be reunited. Occasionally, chips fail so it is worth asking your vet to scan your cat at his annual check-up, to ensure it's still working properly, but the failure rate is very low and chipping has proved to be a very easy, reliable form of identification.

In addition, a collar and tag is useful so your kitten can be returned to you without a scanner and if it is made of reflective material, it could help improve your kitten's visibility in low light.

It is very important that the collar is a safe one and will not strangle your kitten if it is caught on anything. A breakaway collar that snaps open under pressure is a good option.

Scratching post

Scratching is an important part of feline behavior. Expecting a kitten not to scratch is totally unreasonable, but scratching needn't be a problem—as long as you provide him with suitable places to scratch. If he has a scratching post that is the right material, the right height, and in the right place, then he'll have no need to put his claws anywhere near your sofa. Two or three posts should be sufficient for most homes, but you may need more if you have more than one cat, especially if they don't go outside very much.

Avoid carpet-covered scratching boards and posts— your kitten might associate the material with the

action and then begin scratching your rugs. Sisal is therefore preferable.

Toys

A good selection of toys is vital. You must spend time regularly playing with your kitten. This will not only strengthen your relationship, but you'll also be helping to keep him active and stimulated (if bored, he will seek amusement by climbing your curtains, "hunting" your shoelaces, etc). Plus, playing with a kitten is simply great fun and a fabulous way of de-stressing!

The range of toys available these days is astonishing, with everything from fishing-rod type toys and balls with bells to remote-controlled mice and multi-toy activity centers. There is something to suit every puss—and purse!

Whatever toys you buy, don't make every one constantly available to your kitten. To keep his interest in them, put them away, and bring out a couple every day for him to play with. The next day, swap them with different toys. Rotating his toys will help to retain their novelty value for longer.

Also remember that toys don't play themselves. Giving him a toy mouse might amuse him for a few minutes, but he'll soon lose interest if it's not

wiggled to attract his attention, or thrown for him to chase and "hunt."

Feliway

Scent is very important to cats and kittens, not only as a means of communication to other cats but also in terms of his own personal sense of security. If a home smells of his own scent, he will feel far safer than in a new home where there are unfamiliar scents. Kittens put their own smells on objects by rubbing their scent glands against them, particularly facial glands. This is why a kitten will rub his head against the side of furniture, your legs, or against your hand while he is being petted.

Before you bring your new kitten home, put a **pheromone** diffuser (Feliway) in his room, and leave it on continuously for at least four weeks after he arrives. This will reassure him and really help him to feel secure.

Litter Box Training

Kittens take to litter box training remarkably quickly. They are very clean creatures, and, if you give them the right materials in the right places, they will pretty much train themselves! Put a litter box in a quiet corner of the house (in the cat room you have prepared for him), put him in it after he has eaten, and usually that's it. Job done!

If he does have accidents, then there's a reason why. Is the box too close to his bed or food bowls? Understandably, kittens don't like to toilet near where they sleep or eat. Perhaps the litter isn't pleasant for him to walk on (some kittens don't like, for example, the wood-type pellets and prefer a fine-grain litter).

Maybe there's not enough privacy and he doesn't feel secure to go—perhaps because it's too busy and people are coming and going, or he's being stalked by another cat when at his most vulnerable.

Make sure there are plenty of boxes dotted around the house in a multi-cat household, and make sure the boxes are in quiet corners and not busy thoroughfares.

Is the box clean? Would you like to use a dirty bathroom? Neither would a cat! If you don't scoop poop promptly and change the litter regularly, the kitten will find a cleaner place to relieve himself—such as a quiet spot behind your sofa.

If your kitten suddenly becomes incontinent, or, despite your best efforts, continues to have accidents, you must get him seen by a vet, as there may be an underlying health problem.

If your kitten does have an accident, it is vital that the area is cleaned thoroughly, as he will otherwise be attracted back to the area to repeat his performance! An ordinary household cleaner, even bleach, vinegar, or baking soda, will not do the job. Even if the area smells clean to you, the kitten's sensitive nose will pick up any trace of scent .

Use a cleaning product made specifically to clean animal urine. Of course, you should do this cleaning routine on a small, unnoticeable part of the surface first, to check that it is safe to continue.

If your kitten returns to the area out of habit, then move the furniture around so he can't get to the same spot again—or try putting a litter box right on that spot

Note: Pregnant women and those with compromised immune systems should always wear gloves to scoop and clean the litter box, because of the small risk of Toxoplasmosis, a parasitic disease that can be passed on via animal feces.

Family Introductions

Introducing a kitten to an existing cat is often much easier than bringing in a new adult cat, because the youngster is immature and therefore not considered a threat. Two kittens will be as easy to introduce as one, and they will run each other ragged and leave your adult cat alone. It goes without saying that the adult cats should be neutered.

The sex of the cats is not as important as their personalities, activity levels, how they are introduced, and making sure every kitten/cat has enough space and access to important resources (bed, food, litter box, and you!).

Give your new kitten a cat-safe room. Get him settled in this room, door shut initially, so he doesn't venture out—and your existing cat doesn't venture in!

Get the cat and kitten used to each other's scent before they even meet. Smell is very important to cats, and it is helpful if they are familiar with each other's scent before meeting in the flesh.

Stroke one cat, paying particular attention to the cheeks/sides of the mouth, and then go and stroke the other cat. Swapping their blankets/beds is another way of intermingling their scents, as is moving the new kitten out of his room for a short time while the resident cat explores his den.

Welcome home—bringing a new cat into your family.

For a face-to-face meeting, it's important that first impressions are good ones, and that there is no chance of the two fighting or chasing/fleeing. Using a puppy training crate is one option. Put the kitten's bed and litter box inside, cover the top of the crate with a blanket, so it's cosy and den-like, and then let the resident cat investigate. The cats will be able to see and interact with each other—safely. A Feliway diffuser in the room may help to promote calmness.

If you don't have access to a crate, a cat carrier can be used for short, supervised introductions, but the kitten shouldn't be left inside for more than a few minutes.

If the cats ignore each other, great! If there is any signs of aggression, distract them and then reward any calm behavior with some tasty chicken or a similar treat.

Feed the cats in the same room. Time the first few "free" meetings for just before a meal, so both cats are hungry and likely to concentrate on their meals, not each other. Make sure there is plenty of space between them—feeding them in opposite sides of the room and ideally in high-up locations, such as on a table/windowsill/cupboard, so they feel safe.

After a few of these introductions, the novelty of the other will probably wear off and you can let them loose in the house to choose where they spend their time and how they interact.

Canine friends

Only you will know if your dog is cat-friendly. If he gets very excited when he sees cats, then you must get him properly assessed by a **behaviorist** before even thinking about introducing a kitten to your home. Terriers and sighthounds have a particularly high **prey-drive**—after all, they were bred for generations to hunt small, furry, fast-moving animals—and although many can live happily with cats, extra-special care should be taken to ensure they are well-socialized to cats and are introduced and supervised closely.

Install a baby gate in the door of the cat room, so that puss can come out if he chooses to, but the dog cannot hassle him.

Once puss is settled in his room and feels secure and confident, then think about introducing him to the dog. First, introduce their scent (the same way you do scent-swapping with two cats), and swap bedding.

For a face-to-face meeting, it's important that they get their relationship off on a the right foot, with no chasing.

If a dog learns that he can make a kitten run, your cat is at risk of forever being viewed as a great toy—whose batteries never run out! So, after the dog has had a walk, keep him on a leash and arrange for a friend or family member to bring your kitten into the room, placing him on a high spot where he feels safe and the dog cannot reach him. Here he will be able to observe the dog from a distance. Reward the dog if he looks away and ignores your kitten; if he shows interest, distract him calmly.

Short, frequent introductions of this sort will soon get both pets used to the sight of each other and the novelty will wear off.

A training crate can also be used (as for the kitten-to-cat introductions).

When the pets are ready for "free" meetings, off-leash, make sure there are plenty of elevated escape routes for the kitten, so he doesn't need to dash away at floor level if threatened. Hopping up to a high surface is preferable, as it doesn't instigate a chase.

Never leave the kitten and dog unsupervised.

If you need help, don't hesitate to contact a reputable animal behaviorist/trainer. If you get the feline-canine relationship off to a good start they might end up being best buddies.

Outdoors or In?

A kitten should not go outside until he is spayed or neutered and has completed all his vaccinations—so typically at about six months of age. But think carefully about whether you need to let your kitten go outdoors at all. A cat roaming free outside is inevitably exposed to many dangers—from traffic, from curiosity (which might cause them to be shut in other people's houses, sheds, or garages), from poisons in people's gardens or garbage or cars, or from eating a mouse or rat that has ingested toxins, and from other animals, including other cats, dogs, and wild animals (some of which will eat your kitten and all of which will fight if they feel threatened).

We also know that the world is not full of cat lovers, and some people may throw things at your kitten, or try to harm him in other ways—especially if he is annoying them. Your neighbors might not appreciate your kitten coming onto their property, digging and eliminating in their garden, hanging out on their car or deck, coming up to their windows and doors and upsetting their cats and dogs.

In many municipalities, it is illegal to let your cat roam. While these laws are typically not enforced, if your cat is picked up, you will have to pay a hefty fine to get him back—if you get him back at all. Your kitten is your pet and your responsibility, and needs to stay on your property.

Does this mean he can never enjoy the great outdoors? Not at all. What it means is that it's not responsible to simply open the door in the morning, let your kitten out, and remind him to be home before dark. Cats should enjoy the great outdoors the same way dogs and toddlers do: in a safely fenced yard, with human supervision.

Humane societies agree that the only way to let a kitten out is to first safely cat fence your yard, or to build a se-cure enclosure in a part of your yard. Cat-safe fencing goes into the ground and curls inward on top, so your kitten can't climb the fence and escape. There are also a variety of clever outdoor enclosures (catios!) you can

build for a kitten, ranging from a simple screened-in porch to an elaborate enclosed playpen.

If your kitten is outside in the yard or in an enclosure, always make sure he has access to fresh water and a suitable area away from his resting and play places to eliminate. He'll need both shade and sun, and a way to get safely inside if it starts to rain or if something scares him. (If you're outside with him, as you should be, you are his way to get inside.)

If you do let your kitten out in the yard, you'll need to have a way to quickly call him to you. It's really simple to teach a kitten to come. Every day, take out the bag of cat treats, shake it until he comes, and then feed him a few treats. The sound of the shaking bag is now his cue to come to you. Do not let your kitten out, even into a well-fenced yard, until you know you can reliably call him back to you. Then, use this cue every day to call your kitten to you to come inside. This way, coming in doesn't mean the fun is over—it means a treat is coming!

Increasingly, cats are the pets of choice for people who live in cities. If you don't have a yard, does that mean your kitten can't go out? He can! Many cats have learned to walk on a leash and harness. You may have even seen cats on a leash in your city. If you start them out as kittens, they are likely to love it.

- Let the kitten choose the direction he walks in; don't expect him to heel like a dog. You can encourage him with occasional treats.

- If you live in a busy street, pick a time when things are quiet and less busy for your kitten's walks.

- Pay attention to your kitten's body language. He will tell you if he's feeling stressed or scared. Look for flattened ears, body low to the ground, meowing, or nervous tail twitching. If your kitten is not having a good time, take him inside.

- Make sure your kitten doesn't become an escape artist. Some kittens may wait by the door and bolt outside whenever it is opened. Make it clear to your kitten that the only time he can go outside is when he is dressed in his harness. Keep a little bowl of toys near the door, and throw one into the house just before you open the door; when your kitten chases it, you can safely open the door.

Cats who go outdoors have very different vaccination and parasite control needs than do indoor-only cats, so be sure to tell your veterinarian if your kitten goes out, even on leash walks.

House cats

Many people keep their cats permanently indoors, with no loss of welfare for the cat. With a house cat, you have to work extra hard to ensure all your puss's needs are met. If he is deprived of opportunities to express his natural behavior—hunting, climbing, scratching, and all the rest—he will become bored and unhappy, and serious behavior problems can result.

Is he sociable? Would he enjoy a feline playmate? A second kitten can be a great companion.

Play with him as much as you can throughout the day, using a variety of toys to maintain his interest. Set aside time for regular training sessions, too. Cats are very intelligent and take well to training methods that are based in positive rewards, such as clicker training.

Using his brain will keep him mentally alert—plus it's fun and strengthens the pet/owner bond. Give him work to do by feeding his dry kibble only from food-dispenser toys. These are toys your cat must manipulate to get the food out. There's nothing more natural—or more satisfying—for a cat than working to get his food!

Indoor grass is a must for a house cat. Cats enjoy nibbling grass and it's thought to provide essential roughage to prevent constipation and prevent hair-balls. You can bring in other items from the outdoors as well, such as large sticks and branches with fresh leaves—as long as you know they have not been sprayed with pesticides.

The Find Out More section of this book also contains resources for ways you can make your indoor cat's life more interesting, stimulating, and satisfying.

Behavior

Cats are straightforward creatures and rarely have behavioral problems, provided they are raised well, thoroughly socialized, and their basic needs are met. With a kitten, early handling and positive, happy experiences with many different people is very important, as is exposure to different sights and sounds (such as the washing machine, children, friendly dogs, and so on). Make sure the kitten always feels secure, and has an escape route if he feels overwhelmed, and he will learn that he is not in danger.

I f behavioral problems develop, in many cases it's simply a case of understanding why the kitten is behaving as he is (perhaps he is being destructive due to boredom, for example), and providing him with what he is lacking (in this case, more varied, stimulating play and opportunities to exercise his mind and body).

But if you are unable to deal with a problem, do not hesitate to contact an expert, because behavior issues can escalate quickly. The sooner a difficulty is dealt with, the better!

Your vet will first check that there is no underlying health issue responsible for the problem, before referring you to a suitable expert—one who is qualified and experienced in dealing with cat behavior in a kind, non-punitive, reward-based manner.

Why cats act the way they do

Food

Most kittens will eat whatever they are given although some are certainly fussy, especially if you indulge them by replacing perfectly fine cat food with succulent chicken or tuna the moment a kitten, for whatever reason, isn't interested in finishing his meal. It doesn't take long for a canny cat to realize that refusing a meal results in finer fare being offered!

The best advice is to continue feeding whatever he is used to—so ask the breeder or rescue center for diet details. A sudden change in diet can cause diarrhea, and this, together with the stress of a new house and settling in with a new family, can put considerable strain on his body. If you want to change the kitten's diet, wait at least a few weeks, until he's settled, and do it gradually, over the course of a week to 10 days, replacing a little of the cat's old food with the new type, until, eventually, the switch is complete.

Types of diet

There is now a type and flavor of food to suit every taste and budget, and there are even veterinary diets for specific health issues. Crunching on the hard kibble or dry food can be beneficial to a cat's dental health (as opposed to wet foods that stick to the teeth), and dry foods stay fresh much longer, so they make good snacks for overnight or while you are away at work.

Wet food is smellier, messier but often highly attractive to cats, and is preferable for health reasons. Dry foods are full of carbohydrates, which can lead to obesity. Cats also evolved to get much of their daily water intake from their food.

Wet and dry foods usually come in different lifestage varieties, to meet a cat's changing needs. Kitten food is high in energy and protein, to aid growth and development. Once your kitten is about a year old and fully grown, he will need to move on to an adult formula. There are also foods specifically for indoor and overweight cats.

Feeding times

Dry food can be put out in the morning and left throughout the day for the cat to graze on. Follow the amounts recommended on the package, but adjust according to your kitten's body condition and how hungry he seems. Kittens are small, but they need a lot of food to grow—sometimes more than an adult cat.. Or you can divide his daily amount into two or three portions, which you put down for morning, lunchtime and evening. This might be preferable if you have a multi-cat household where one greedy puss might tuck into other cats' meals if not monitored.

Wet food should not be left out all day, as it will spoil. Your cats might appreciate a schedule of wet food morning and evening, and small amounts of dry food for snacking in between.

Drinks

Fresh drinking water must be available at all times. Some cats prefer running water—many a cat will be found pawing at a dripping tap—and pet drinking fountains are available for such water babies. Cats don't need milk, and some are lactose intolerant. If yours is, you'll see the result in the litter box.

Grass

Kittens and adult cats in the wild do nibble some greens, so it's important to provide some indoors, as the roughage aids digestion, and may help with hairballs. The grass can be grown easily indoors in little tubs for the kitten to graze on.

Grooming

Most shorthaired cats are perfectly equipped to groom themselves. Their rough tongues brush through the coat, distributing natural oils and removing dead hair. But that's not to say they don't need a helping hand. An all-over brushing once a week will help prevent hairballs and minimize the amount of dead hair that is left around the house on carpets, clothing, and furniture. It will also help with the pet-owner bond, and give you the chance to look for any parasites in the coat and for any physical changes that need to be investigated by a vet, such as lumps or scratches.

Some breeds need more assistance, though, particularly where humans have interfered with the original cat design. For example, the Persian's coat is now so long and thick that the cat would not be able to keep it in good condition without human help. A Persian would be a matted mess in a very short time if left to his own devices.

When you buy or adopt your kitten, the breeder or rescue center should give you specific advice on the grooming care that your kitten will need, not just now but when he is fully grown and has his adult coat.

Lookin' good! Cat grooming tips.

Routine

Getting a kitten used to grooming is so important. If he gets used to the experience when young, it will make life much simpler in the future—especially if he's medium or longhaired.

Accustoming him to being brushed and combed is simple if you incorporate it into an ordinary petting session. Stroke him all over and, when he's relaxed and purring, simply begin to brush him gently (keep your grooming tools by your favorite armchair, so they are in easy reach!). Brush for just a minute or two of, give him a treat, and then simply stroke him with your hand again.

Later, try a couple more minutes. Keep sessions short and frequent, and very gradually extend them in terms of time and the areas groomed.

When he has his adult coat, use the services of a professional groomer if you don't have the time or expertise to keep his coat tidy. If your cat would be stressed by the car trip or visit to a salon, find a groomer that will visit your home.

Health

Kittens are usually pretty robust, healthy creatures, with accidents being a chief cause of a visit to the vet (broken bones, eating something he shouldn't, etc). Kitten-proofing your home and close supervision will help to minimize such accidents, but it's advisable to be safety-conscious (see page 48) and prepared for emergencies. Kittens really do seem to have nine lives, managing to get into—and out of—all sorts of scrapes, but that's not to say that they are invincible!

Keep the cat carrier in an easily accessible place (not hidden at the back of the garage under a ton of unused garden furniture or in far recesses of the attic), so you can find it, put the kitten inside, and drive to the vet as quickly as possible if he needs urgent medical treatment.

On the fridge door, by the phone, or somewhere else that's visible and immediately obvious, post the number of your vet clinic, and keep a pen and piece of paper close by in case you need to write down the details of the after-hours emergency contact. Kittens can go downhill quickly, so seek immediate veterinary advice whenever your kitten is less than 100 percent.

Illness

Be alert to signs of illness so you can contact your vet at the earliest opportunity. The sooner this intervention comes, the better the chances of recovery.

Signs of illness are too numerous to list here, but you should be looking out for any change from your cat's usual condition and normal behavior. If he's sleepier than usual, drinking or eating more or less, if he's grooming more, if he's grumpy or less tolerant of being petted. All of these signs can suggest that something is wrong. More obvious signs are the physical changes: perhaps there's a change in the type and frequency of his toileting habits; perhaps there's a change to his coat, his eyes and/or nose are runny, or he's scratching himself. Has he lost or put on weight? Does his breath smell? Have any lumps appeared?

All of these signs can be spotted quickly if you spend time with your kitten, and instinct often kicks in, too. "I can't put my finger on it, but my pet just doesn't seem himself" is commonly heard at vet practices around the country, and, from there, the vet can examine the kitten and make a diagnosis.

Do not ever be tempted to treat the kitten yourself. Many drugs intended for humans are highly toxic to cats. A visit to the professionals at the first sign of illness often means a condition can be treated quickly—and more affordably.

Pet insurance is worth exploring, as unexpected vet bills can be difficult—particularly if, given veterinary advances, specialist treatment is needed or a chronic, long-term condition emerges. Do be aware of the different types of policies when researching insurance, as different policies offer different types of coverage.

Spay and neuter

Neutering involves removing the testes in males and spaying is taking out the ovaries and uterus in females. Neutering your cat is essential, to avoid unwanted pregnancies and to protect his or his health. When so many perfectly healthy cats and kittens are being destroyed for want of a home, breeding a litter of random breeds is unforgivable. Even if you have homes for the anticipated kittens, by producing a litter, you will be condemning to death shelter cats that could have been rescued instead.

Neutering a cat will also prevent spraying in toms, calling in **queens** and will prevent them acquiring sexually transmitted diseases. **Toms** often fight when competing for a mate, too, and are then at risk of diseases such as calicivirus, FIV, and feline leukaemia, for example. Unneutered cats are at increased risk of road accidents, too.

If your kitten isn't already neutered when you adopt him/her, it's imperative that he is kept away from any unneutered cats of the opposite sex. Your vet will advise you of the best time, depending on your specific circumstances, but it is generally done at around six months.

Vacations

When you go away, you can't just leave your kitten alone at home with a pile of dry food and some toys. He's a social animal, and needs company. He also needs to be checked on daily. However, it's not unusual for a neighbor to happily volunteer to stop by, feed him, clean the litter box, and give him a cuddle for a few days. It's far less stressful for the kitten to be in his home environment.

If the friend/neighbor option isn't possible, you could pay a professional pet-sitter to come in and care for the kitten a couple of times a day, or even to live in your home while you're away if you'd prefer and can afford this luxury. Do make sure you go through a reputable agency and check up on the sitter's references. It's also advisable to meet the person before you go away, to talk through the cat's specific needs and routines, and to ensure you are happy to entrust

Bad combo—cats and Christmas trees!

your home and loved one to them. If you are not 100 percent satisfied, ask the agency for another sitter.

A third option is a cattery. If a kitten has been used to going to a cattery from a young age, he could well be happy with such an arrangement, though most cats, if given the option, would prefer the comfort of home. Check out the cattery carefully, visiting the premises, talking to the staff and asking lots of questions about their experience, the cats' care arrangements, and so on. Your cat will have to be fully vaccinated to be accepted, so make sure you have the necessary boosters done in time for them to be effective—and have the right paperwork to show as proof.

Find Out More

Books

Bradshaw, John. *Cat Sense*. Basic Books, 2014.

Delzio, Suzanne, and Cindy Ribarich. *Felinestein: Pampering the Genius in Your Cat*. Harper, 1999.

Johnson-Bennett, Pam. *Think Like a Cat*. Penguin, 2011.

Raindolt, Dusty. *Kittens for Dummies*. Wiley, 2011.

Web Sites

indoorpet.osu.edu/cats/
The Indoor Pet Initiative, from Ohio State University Veterinary School, has everything you need to know to keep an indoor cat happy.

www.youtube.com/user/ PositiveCattitudes?feature=mhum
This is the YouTube channel of a very talented cat clicker trainer, to get you started training your cat.

www.catbehaviorassociates.com
Get cat behavior advice from one of the world's top cat behavior consultants.

 **Words to Understand**

behaviorist   a person who studies animal behavior

domesticated   an animal who has been bred to live with people, as a pet or on a farm

pedigree   the family tree of a purebred animal; a cat with a pedigree is pedigreed

pheromone   a chemical substance produced by an animal that affects the behavior of other animals

prey-drive   a strong instinct to hunt other animals for food

queen   a female cat who has not been spayed

socialize   the process of teaching your cat about the world he lives in, so that he does not feel frightened, alarmed, or threatened when he encounters new situations and new experiences

tom   a male cat who has not been neutered

toxic   poisonous; deadly to living things

Index

African wildcat 16

Asian leopard cat 26

Bengal 26

breeds 24-38

Burmese 30

choosing a kitten 40, 42

dogs and kittens 53, 78, 80

Egypt 18

equipment 56, 57, 58, 59

food 57, 102, 103, 104, 106

gender, determining 46, 47

grass 107

grooming 110, 111, 112

health 116, 117, 118, 119

history 16, 18

house cat issues 92, 94

identification 59, 60

insurance 119

Isle of Man 32

kitten-proofing 50, 52, 53

litter box training 68, 70, 72

Maine Coon Cat 28

Manx 32

Middle Ages 18

mixed breed 38

number of kittens 22, 23, 74, 75, 76

outdoor cats 84, 86, 88, 90

Panthera 16

Pet Food Manufacturer's Association 13

Persian 36

safe room 50

scratching post 60

sealpoint Siamese 30

Siamese 34, 36

spay and neuter 120

Thailand (Siam) 30, 34

toys 62

vacation car 124, 125

witches 18